RAINFOREST

DISCOVER THE EXTRAORDINARY LIFE IN EARTH'S MOST DELICATE ECOSYSTEMS

WRITTEN BY
DR. MICHAEL LEACH AND DR. MERIEL LLAND

CONSULTANT DEREK HARVEY

DK Penguin Random House

DK LONDON
Senior Editor Michelle Crane
Senior Art Editor Rachael Grady
Managing Editor Francesca Baines
Managing Art Editor Philip Letsu
US Senior Editor Jennette ElNaggar
Production Editor Gillian Reid
Senior Production Controller Leanne Burke
Senior Jacket Designer Rashika Kachroo
Managing Art Editor (Jackets) Romi Chakraborty
Publisher Andrew Macintyre
Art Director Mabel Chan

Illustrators Andrew Beckett (Illustration X),
Chris@KJA, Sofian Moumene

First American Edition, 2025
Published in the United States by DK Publishing,
a division of Penguin Random House LLC
1745 Broadway, 20th Floor, New York, NY 10019

Copyright © 2025 Dorling Kindersley Limited
A Penguin Random House Company
25 26 27 28 29 10 9 8 7 6 5 4 3 2 1
001–344913–Apr/2025

A catalog record for this book
is available from the Library of Congress.
ISBN 978-0-5939-6455-2

Printed and bound in China

www.dk.com

CONTENTS

4 ANCIENT WORLD

6 CROWDED CANOPY

8 THE WILDS OF ALASKA

10 AFTER DARK

12 A WATERY WORLD

14 A PRIMATES' PLAYGROUND

16 HIGH-RISE LIVING

18 ENCHANTED ISLAND

20 UP IN THE CLOUDS

22 FALLEN GIANT

24 ISOLATED WORLD

26 FAIRY-TALE FOREST

28 THE FLOODED FOREST

30 RAINFOREST PLANTS
AND FUNGI

32 MULTILAYERED HABITAT,
GLOSSARY, AND INDEX

KEY
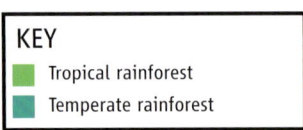
■ Tropical rainforest
■ Temperate rainforest

EARTH'S RAINFORESTS

A rainforest is a forest that receives more than 118 in (3,000 mm) of rain each year. Tropical rainforests are hot and humid and grow near the equator. Temperate rainforests thrive in cooler areas. Rainforests contain more than half of all plant and animal species, despite covering only 2 to 6 percent of the Earth.

TONGASS NATIONAL FOREST

Alaska, US (see pages 8–9)
Tongass is the Earth's largest remaining temperate rainforest. It is a coastal rainforest with mild weather conditions and high rainfall. The trees are mostly coniferous—including cedar and spruce.

NORTH AMERICA

MONTEVERDE CLOUD FOREST RESERVE

Costa Rica (see pages 20–21)
This reserve is high in a range of mountains where the forest canopy is often hidden in low-hanging dense cloud. Plants here take life-giving moisture from rain or directly from the clouds.

SOUTH AMERICA

MANÚ NATIONAL PARK

Peru (see pages 12–13)
Manú National Park has a range of fascinating rainforest habitats, from hot lowland to cool montane. Its diverse landscape is home to more than 1,000 species of birds and 200 mammal species.

IQUITOS VÁRZEA

Brazil (see pages 28–29)
Huge areas of the western Amazon rainforest flood every year during the wet season—this is called floodplain rainforest or várzea. Rivers overflow and some of the forest lies underwater for a time.

LOMAMI NATIONAL PARK
**Democratic Republic of the Congo
(see pages 22–23)**
Lomami National Park is part of a vast tropical, lowland rainforest that once covered most of Central Africa.

VOLCANOES NATIONAL PARK
Rwanda (see pages 14–15)
This park lies on the steep slopes of five volcanoes that include montane—or mountain—rainforest. Montane rainforest is cool and frequently shrouded in thick cloud.

YAKUSHIMA NATIONAL PARK
Japan (see pages 26–27)
An ancient evergreen rainforest with warm-temperate conditions, this park is rich with huge Yakushima cedars. Located on an island, its trees are never felled. Temperatures vary little over the year.

EUROPE

ASIA

AFRICA

Tropic of Cancer

TANJUNG PUTING NATIONAL PARK
Borneo, Indonesia (see pages 6–7)
Hot and humid throughout the year, the park is one of the largest protected habitats in Southeast Asia. It is a coastal, tropical lowland rainforest with many swampy areas.

Equator

BOUMA NATIONAL HERITAGE PARK
**Taveuni Island, Fiji
(see pages 24–25)**
One of the world's most remote tropical, coastal rainforests thrives on Taveuni Island in the Pacific Ocean. It has fewer species than some forests, but its inhabitants are unique.

OCEANIA

Tropic of Capricorn

DAINTREE
Queensland, Australia (see pages 4–5)
The oldest rainforest on Earth, Daintree is part of the largest continuous area of wet, tropical rainforest in Australia. Today, it is home to many primitive plants and ancient animal species.

MAKIRA NATURAL PARK
Madagascar (see pages 10–11)
Makira's humid rainforests receive less rain than many lowland forests. This is the largest protected area in Madagascar. Separated from Africa about 160 million years ago, the island features extraordinary wildlife.

TAMAN NEGARA NATIONAL PARK
Malaysia (see pages 16–17)
This park features diverse tropical rainforest habitats including lowland dipterocarp forests. Dipterocarps are a family of giant, hardwood trees that can grow to 197 ft (60 m).

RAKIURA NATIONAL PARK
Stewart Island/Rakiura, New Zealand (see pages 18–19)
Rakiura is a remnant of the temperate hardwood rainforest that covered much of New Zealand before humans arrived 1,000 years ago. Temperate means the climate is neither too hot nor too cold.

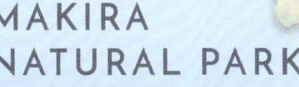

ANTARCTICA

4

The colorful *rose-crowned fruit dove* often drinks rainwater from leaves, and is especially fond of figs. It swallows fruits whole, and its droppings disperse seeds.

Saltwater crocodiles are the world's biggest reptiles. The largest stay close to the sea, but younger, smaller crocodiles often explore Daintree's rivers.

Elephant foot yams are susceptible to sunburn. They grow well in the understory in the shade of blue quandong trees.

Green-eyed tree frogs stay close to water. Females lay their eggs under rocks in streams to protect them from predators.

Bumpy satinash tree

Lace monitor

Azure kingfisher

Northern pencil orchid

Whipbird

Duck-billed platypus

Cassowary chick

Rainbow stag beetle

Velvet leaf

Southern cassowaries are flightless birds that eat fruit. They defend themselves with powerful kicks and a lethal daggerlike claw. The male raises the chicks alone.

Part bird, part rodent? The *duck-billed platypus* is actually neither! It is a monotreme—a mammal that lays eggs instead of giving birth to live young.

Male *satin bowerbirds* build complex stick structures called bowers to attract females. They decorate the bowers with blue objects such as berries, feathers, and shells.

Boyd's forest dragons are arboreal—or tree dwelling. They look out for insects from their high perch and scurry to the ground to catch them.

Also known as dinosaur trees, *idiot fruit trees* are relics of the ancient rainforest. Their seeds are so toxic that nothing eats them.

The *lichen huntsman spider* resembles lichen. It can be difficult to spot against a tree.

Wild banana

Fan palm

Giant blue earthworm

ANCIENT WORLD
Daintree, Queensland, Australia

Daintree is the oldest wet tropical rainforest on Earth, emerging 180 million years ago. Dinosaurs once roamed under its emerald canopy, but today their descendants, including southern cassowaries—primitive birds with three-toed feet—can be spotted among the giant fan palms and prehistoric plants.

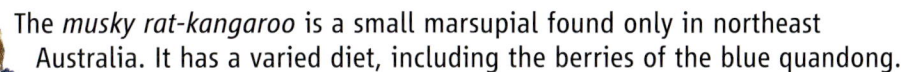
The *musky rat-kangaroo* is a small marsupial found only in northeast Australia. It has a varied diet, including the berries of the blue quandong.

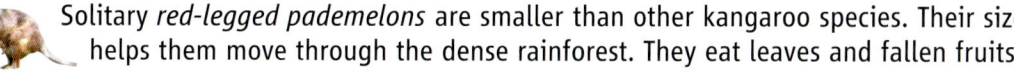
Solitary *red-legged pademelons* are smaller than other kangaroo species. Their size helps them move through the dense rainforest. They eat leaves and fallen fruits.

Sun bears have a remarkably long tongue for licking honey and grubs from bees' nests. They are good climbers and sometimes rest in trees.

Bees build nests in emergent trees and help pollinate the forest. *Blue-throated bee-eaters* hunt for swarms and feed on the bees.

Whiskered treeswifts catch flying insects by darting out briefly while watching for prey from their canopy perches.

Clouded leopards are skilled predators. They hunt on the forest floor and in the canopy—this one is stalking the binturong.

Rajah Brooke's birdwing butterfly

White-bellied woodpecker

Crested serpent eagle

CROWDED CANOPY
Tanjung Puting National Park, Borneo, Indonesia

At dawn, the steamy lowland rainforest awakens with a powerful chorus of calls and birdsong—each animal looking for breakfast or establishing territory. As the new day begins, the hidden life of the canopy ecosystem is revealed. This is where sunlight permeates, allowing photosynthesis. Flowers bloom, fruits ripen, primates bask in sunshine, butterflies and bees fly over the trees, and one of the world's largest population of orangutans makes their home.

Binturong

Male orangutan

A male orangutan is breakfasting on red-fleshed *durian*, a favorite food of orangutans. Although durian fruit tastes of caramel and vanilla, it's notorious for its horrible smell.

The enormous noses of male *proboscis monkeys* pump up the volume of their honking calls. The monkeys forage widely for leaves but return to their riverside home at night.

Large *flying foxes* are actually bats. They were named "foxes" because of their doglike faces. They roost in colonies and feed on fruit, flowers, and nectar.

A young *orangutan* lives with its mother for up to 10 years. She shows the infant how to survive and thrive in this complex rainforest environment.

Menggaris tree

Rhinoceros hornbill

The tallest orchid in the world, the *tiger orchid* is an epiphyte—it can grow to more than 23 ft (7 m) in height.

The *jasper cat snake* feeds at night on geckos and birds. This one is heading away to rest and digest its prey.

Wallace's flying frog does not actually fly. It glides or parachutes between branches using huge, webbed feet that it splays to catch the air.

The *banded flower mantis* is very skilled at camouflage. Disguised against forest flowers, these ambush predators wait for passing butterflies or other insects.

The *red-breasted sapsucker's* tongue has stiff hairs for collecting sap. It drills neat holes in trees and waits for the sap to flow.

The main prey of *Alexander Archipelago wolves* are Sitka black-tailed deer, but salmon may provide up to 25 percent of their diet.

Witch's hair is a lichen that grows strung over conifer tree branches. It has no roots but takes nutrients from the air and rain.

Salmonberries are eaten by birds and bears. The plants' seeds are then distributed throughout the forest in droppings.

Great horned owl

Black bear

Prince of Wales spruce grouse

Goatsbeard

Haida ermine

Long-distance migrants, *rufous hummingbirds* breed here then fly down to Mexico for winter—a circuit of 2,000 miles (3,200 km). They feed on western columbine nectar.

Western skunk cabbage produces a very unpleasant scent that attracts flies and beetles. The bugs pollinate the flowers, while the plant feeds deer and black bears.

Living up to 800 years, *Sitka spruce* can reach a height of 330 ft (100 m). They have shallow roots and can be toppled by strong winds.

 For much of the year, *Sitka brown bears* mostly eat plants. But during the salmon run, they feast on protein-rich fish ahead of hibernation.

THE WILDS OF ALASKA
Tongass National Forest, Alaska, US

Something astonishing happens every summer in this remote, temperate rainforest. Silently, bears and wolves emerge from the mossy, cedar-scented woods to wait at the waterside. A flash of pink breaks the river's surface. This is the time of the "salmon run," when millions of fish leave the Pacific Ocean and swim inland to breed. They are easy prey for hungry predators preparing for winter.

Golden-crowned kinglet

Western red hemlock

Bald eagles are specialized fish-eaters and snatch salmon from the water with their sharp, powerful talons.

Although called *river otters*, these inquisitive animals are happy on land or in water. They often play with sticks or small stones.

Chicken of the woods fungus

Devil's club

Sitka black-tailed deer

Northern goshawk

Western water shrew

American dipper

 Dark green clumps of *western sword fern* emerge from the springy mosses and leaf litter. Their fronds can grow up to 6 ft (180 cm) tall.

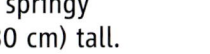 *Sockeye salmon* spend most of their life in the ocean but return to their freshwater birthplace to spawn, dying shortly after. Their bodies supply nutrients to feed the rainforest.

Indri, one of the largest lemurs, live in small family groups. They communicate by roaring and singing together. These complex "concerts" help defend territory.

Shy *aye-ayes* are long-fingered lemurs with especially thin middle fingers used to probe trees in search of grubs. Local folklore suggests aye-ayes bring bad luck.

AFTER DARK
Makira Natural Park, Madagascar

Isolated for millions of years, 90 percent of Madagascar's plants and animals exist only on this wild island. Daylight hours reveal singing lemurs and giraffe-necked weevils. After dark, the humid lowland rainforest is haunted by even stranger creatures—meet the eerie aye-aye, the satanic leaf-tailed gecko, and the menacing fossa.

Blue coua

Nelicourvi weaver

The endangered *helmet vanga* lives only in undisturbed humid rainforest on Madagascar. It snatches up insects with its big bill.

Catat's palm

Traveller's tree

Crested drongo

Ring-tailed vontsira

Panther chameleon

The "wings" of the female *long-winged kite spider* are not for flying but part of her spiny body. The spines deter predators.

Bird's nest fern

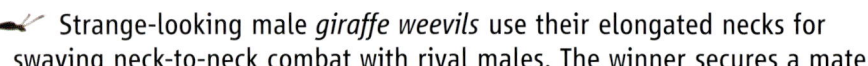

Strange-looking male *giraffe weevils* use their elongated necks for swaying neck-to-neck combat with rival males. The winner secures a mate.

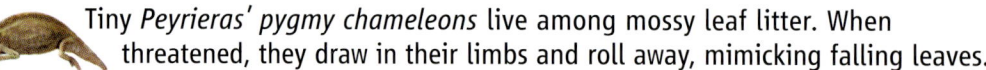

Tiny *Peyrieras' pygmy chameleons* live among mossy leaf litter. When threatened, they draw in their limbs and roll away, mimicking falling leaves.

Catlike *fossas* are the largest carnivorous mammal in Madagascar. When hunting at night, their eyes reflect light, making them glow orange.

Lowland streaked tenrecs use their sensitive noses to hunt out earthworms. Their quills vibrate to communicate with young or deter predators such as the fossa.

Masoala fork-marked lemurs are skilled at extracting gum that oozes from insect holes made in trees.

Dung beetles are superb recyclers. They roll up and bury balls of dung for food and as breeding chambers for their young.

Madagascar flying fox

Madagascar scops owl

Cynorkis peyrotii

Madagascan moon moth

Bright-eyed frog

Malagasy net-casting spider

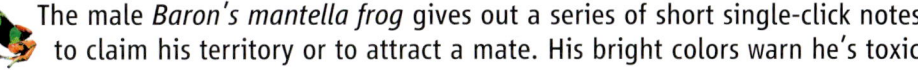
The male *Baron's mantella frog* gives out a series of short single-click notes to claim his territory or to attract a mate. His bright colors warn he's toxic.

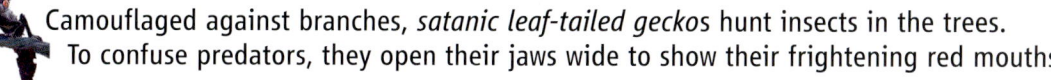
Camouflaged against branches, *satanic leaf-tailed geckos* hunt insects in the trees. To confuse predators, they open their jaws wide to show their frightening red mouths.

Peruvian spider monkeys have prehensile tails that act as a fifth limb or hand. They use them to grab branches and even collect food.

The upper sides of the *blue morpho butterfly's* wings are bright blue. The wings close when a predator approaches and show only a camouflaged brown underside.

A WATERY WORLD
Manú National Park, Peru

The heart of the tropical Amazon rainforest is the river. Where the canopy is broken, on its banks and underwater, it bursts with wildlife. In April, as wet season floodwaters recede, caimans, otters, and anacondas come to hunt piranha. Capybaras and tapirs feed on lush vegetation, while afternoon skies fill with flitting parrots and macaws.

Giant otters are top predators of the river. Their main food is fish, but they will also hunt snakes and young caimans.

The yellow spots on a *yellow-spotted turtle's* head are visible when the turtles are young but fade with age.

Aguaje palm

Squirrel monkey

Scarlet macaw

Red-and-green macaw

South American tapir

Spectacled caiman

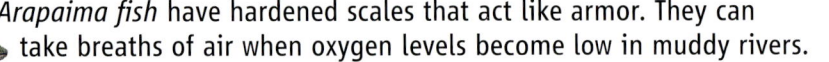

Arapaima fish have hardened scales that act like armor. They can take breaths of air when oxygen levels become low in muddy rivers.

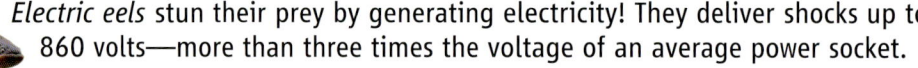

Electric eels stun their prey by generating electricity! They deliver shocks up to 860 volts—more than three times the voltage of an average power socket.

Blue-and-yellow macaws come down to riverbank "clay-licks"—exposed cliffs where they eat clay. Minerals found in the clay neutralize toxins found in the plants they eat.

Capybaras are the world's largest rodents. They live in family groups and are always close to freshwater. They especially enjoy plants that grow underwater.

The stealthy *jaguar* is one of the few cat species that swims well and even plays in water. They hunt young caimans.

Curl-crested aracari

Three-toed sloth

Green anacondas are the world's heaviest snake. They spend much of their lives in water and kill prey by constriction.

Wild fig

Although most piranha species don't live up to their bad reputation, *Red-bellied piranhas* are the most carnivorous and may nip the flesh of other fishes.

Black caimans eat almost any animal smaller than themselves—including other caimans! They cannot chew their food—instead, they swallow it whole.

Rwenzori turacos are heavy birds with relatively small wings. When moving between trees, they glide to save valuable energy instead of using powered flight.

Endangered *mountain gorillas* live in family groups. Gorillas are shy and gentle but enjoy climbing, tumbling, and playing together. They are big plant-eaters.

A PRIMATES' PLAYGROUND
Volcanoes National Park, Rwanda

The Virunga Mountains rise tall and misty, wrapped in tropical montane rainforest. Golden monkeys leap through bamboo groves while mountain gorillas move quietly beyond the hagenia trees in search of food. This magical place is home to conservation projects helping protect these gentle giants. On the subalpine slopes above the rainforest, the huge leaves of megaherbs sway softly in the breeze.

Giant heather

Giant lobelia

African redwood

African cherry

Fern tree

Rare *Virungas golden monkeys* feed on leaves, fruits, and bamboo shoots. They weave nests for sleeping at the top of bamboo stems.

African alpine bamboo is a giant grass with a hollow, strong, woody stem that helps it grow to a height of 65 ft (20 m).

The *handsome spurfowl* is known for its sharp spurs and distinctive calls. It flies only when forced by danger, usually running into cover instead.

Shy and well-camouflaged, the *Kivu ground thrush* lives in the understory of the rainforest. It eats invertebrates as well as fruits and seeds.

Ruwenzori duikers are small antelope only 18 in (45 cm) tall. For defense, both male and female duikers have short, sharp horns.

Little is known about the solitary and secretive *African golden cat*. The dense rainforest provides cover as it stalks prey—such as the Ruwenzori duiker.

Boehm's bush squirrels spend their lives low down on tree trunks and branches, and feed on ants and caterpillars.

Delicious *wild celery* is one of the favorite foods of mountain gorillas. It can reach up to 10 ft (3 m) in height.

Mountain oriole

Giant groundsel

Curry bush

Doherty's bushshrike

African green broadbill

Forest nettle

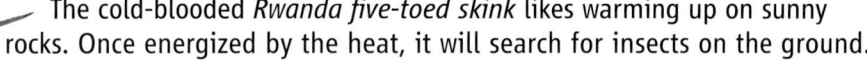
The cold-blooded *Rwanda five-toed skink* likes warming up on sunny rocks. Once energized by the heat, it will search for insects on the ground.

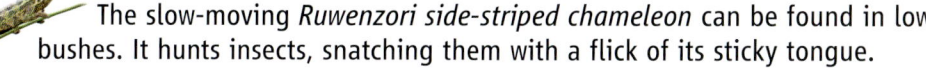
The slow-moving *Ruwenzori side-striped chameleon* can be found in low bushes. It hunts insects, snatching them with a flick of its sticky tongue.

The seeds of the *meranti tree* have a very special dispersal trick. They have "wings" that catch the wind and spin them far away.

Flying dragons are lizards that spend most of their time clinging to vertical tree trunks. Their winglike skin flaps allow them to glide from trunk to trunk.

Crested honey buzzards raid bee and wasp nests for larvae, comb, and honey. Scalelike feathers protect their eyes from stings.

In cross section the delicious, yellow fruit of the wild star fruit tree is star-shaped. The fruits are grown worldwide.

HIGH-RISE LIVING
Taman Negara National Park, Malaysia

It's a steamy afternoon in the rainy season. The tropical lowland rainforest glistens as the shower eases and the sun returns. From the forest floor to the top, different kinds of trees grow to different heights. Giant tualang and meranti trees emerge high above the canopy and host nesting hornbills, flying dragons, and hungry honey buzzards. In their shade, rambutans and pitcher plants thrive. Their nectar and fruits draw in more wildlife. Here, tigers stalk mouse deer and snakes hunt other snakes.

Great hornbill

Ruby-cheeked sunbird

Meranti tree

Prevost's squirrel

Tualang

Red-naped trogon

Crab-eating macaque

The *blue-crowned hanging parrot* likes to eat and sleep upside down. After supper of rambutan fruit, it hangs from branches and roosts like a bat.

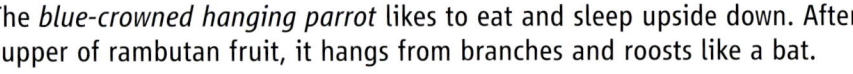
Malaysian lar gibbons can move through the canopy by hanging down and swinging from tree to tree using long, powerful hands to hook onto branches.

Skilled at climbing, the long and slender *elegant bronzeback snake* spends most of its life in the trees. It is hunted by the venomous king cobra.

Corpse flowers are the world's biggest flowers, measuring around 39 in (1 m) across. They have a foul rotting meat smell to attract pollinating flies.

The *white bat flower*, or tiger's whiskers lily, has many common names because of its unusual appearance.

Red junglefowl are ancestors to chickens. Around 8,000 years ago, people began keeping the birds for eggs and slowly domesticated them.

Epiphyte orchid

Mouse deer

King cobra

Gaur

Green land snail

Chestnut breasted malkoha

Malayan tigers have a striped coat that helps camouflage them in the shadowy, dense rainforest. They stalk prey, such as mouse deer, very slowly.

Pitcher plants are carnivorous. They have deep pitfalls that trap insects and other small animals. Inside is a liquid that digests their prey and helps feed the plant.

 Busy, chattering *New Zealand fantails* are almost never still. They zip from twig to twig in the forest understory hunting flying insects.

 *Little blue penguins* are the world's smallest species of penguin. They are skilled at digging nesting burrows if suitable natural sites are unavailable.

New Zealand bellbirds feed on nectar from fuchsia flowers and honeydew, a sticky, sweet liquid produced by scale insects.

ENCHANTED ISLAND
Rakiura National Park, New Zealand

Spring in the temperate rainforest on Stewart Island/Rakiura reveals a largely untouched landscape of lush trees and ferns. A midday-to-midnight glimpse of this special place includes nesting penguins, nocturnal parrots, and scurrying bats. On rare nights, the island is illuminated by the Aurora Australis—the Southern Lights. Rakiura means "glowing skies" in the local Māori language.

Noisy *tūī* birds defend the best feeding sites by driving away intruders with a dipped head and fanned tail.

Tōtara

Red-crowned parakeet

New Zealand pigeon

Saddleback

Brown creeper

South Island tomtit

Kāmahi

Basket fungus

Bush lawyer

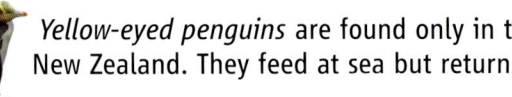 *Yellow-eyed penguins* are found only in the waters around New Zealand. They feed at sea but return to the forest to breed.

 *Shining bronze cuckoos* do not build nests. Females lay eggs in the nests of tomtits and leave them to raise their cuckoo chicks.

Kākāpō, a Māori word for "night parrots," are flightless. Critically endangered, most kākāpō have been relocated to predator-free conservation islands.

Fungi can help decay fallen trees but also damage living ones. Some have a bioluminescent glow to attract insects that carry the spores away.

Astonishing *leaf-veined slugs* have brilliant leaflike markings that help hide them from predators.

Lesser short-tailed bats not only catch moths in the air but also scurry around the rainforest floor hunting spiders and beetles.

Morepork

Fork fern

Rimu

Kaka parrot

Emerald pug moth

Weka

Weta

Flightless *southern brown kiwis* have nostrils at the end of their beaks and an excellent sense of smell that they use to find earthworms and spiders.

Huhus are New Zealand's heaviest beetles. They lay eggs on rotting logs. The larvae—or grubs—bore into dead trees eating decomposing wood.

The extraordinary long tail plumes of male *resplendent quetzals* help attract females during their springtime courtship flights.

Monarch butterflies avoid North American winters by flying south in September. Many come to Monteverde's cloud forests, returning north in spring.

Black guans live in high altitude forests. These heavy, chicken-sized birds nimbly search the canopy for fruit to eat.

Some bromeliads, like *guzmania*, hold rainwater providing treetop pools for aquatic insects and frogs.

Variegated squirrel

White-faced capuchin

Swallow-tailed kite

Costa Rican oak

Wild avocado tree

Coppery-headed emerald

Tillandsia multicaulis

Glasswing butterfly

Leafcutter ants

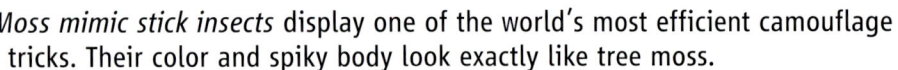
Moss mimic stick insects display one of the world's most efficient camouflage tricks. Their color and spiky body look exactly like tree moss.

Frogs thrive in cloud forests. *Red-eyed tree frogs* lay eggs under wet leaves so hatching tadpoles can drop into pools of water below.

A bone inside the throat of the *golden-mantled howler monkey* amplifies its calls. These territorial roars can be heard up to 2.5 miles (4 km) away.

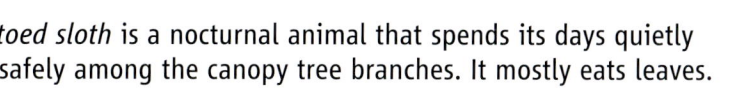

Hoffmann's two-toed sloth is a nocturnal animal that spends its days quietly sleeping, curled safely among the canopy tree branches. It mostly eats leaves.

UP IN THE CLOUDS
Monteverde Cloud Forest Reserve, Costa Rica

It's spring on the mountains above the hot lowland rainforest as clouds drift through the trees thick with lush epiphytes and vines. Conditions are cooler up here and moisture is carried in the air creating a dense fog. In this saturated world, amazing creatures thrive, like the bellbird with its loud territorial calls that echo through the air and the peanut-headed bug with its oddly shaped head. Short spells of sunlight bring the canopy alive with swirling butterflies and noisy monkeys. When the cloud descends again, quiet falls and the forest is still.

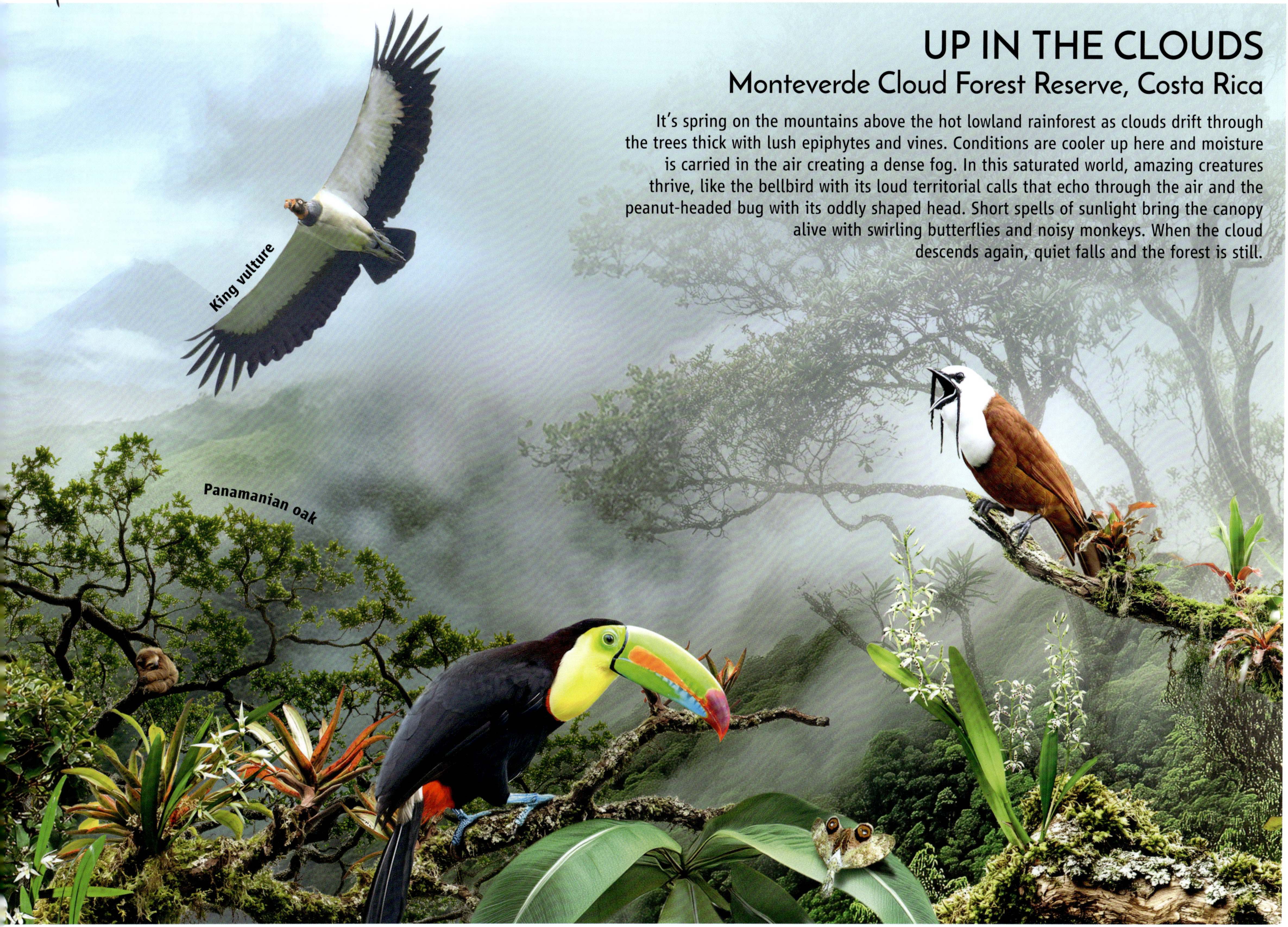

King vulture

Panamanian oak

Like many other epiphytes, the *rainbow orchid* absorbs much of its water directly from the fog-laden air, rather than through roots.

The *keel-billed toucan* breaks open tough seeds with its enormous bill—but tackles soft fruits by tossing them into the air and swallowing them whole.

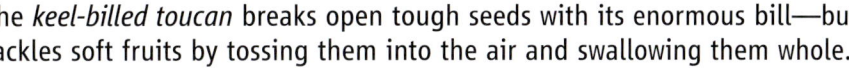

When facing predators, *peanut-headed bugs* open their wings to display fake eyes—called eyespots—that make them look like much bigger animals.

21

Solitary *leopards* are skilled tree-climbers and adaptable hunters. They ambush prey, with antelopes such as the blue duiker being a favorite target.

Golden-bellied mangabeys cover long distances within their home territories in search of food. Liana vines help them travel quickly through the trees.

Forest elephants use their tusks to push through the shrubbery in the understory. Their browsing may cause tree-falls.

African pear saplings are fast-growing and fill the gap in the canopy opened by the fallen tree.

FALLEN GIANT
Lomami National Park, Democratic Republic of the Congo

A violent, afternoon rainy season storm brought down a 400-year-old afrormosia tree in this tropical lowland rainforest. The tree-fall has opened the canopy so light floods in. Seeds germinate, saplings grow, and decay begins. Now fungi and termites are breaking down the wood. Vital nutrients are returning to the soil in a process of sustainable recycling.

African ebony

Blue duiker

Afrormosia tree

Wild cardamom

Bongo

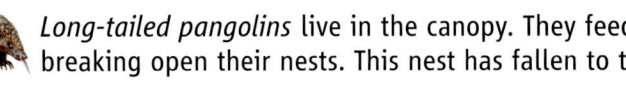
Long-tailed pangolins live in the canopy. They feed on arboreal ants, breaking open their nests. This nest has fallen to the ground in the tree-fall.

Congo peafowl pair for life. They are committed parents and care for their chicks for three months until their offspring become independent.

Bonobos eat a huge variety of fruits and other vegetation, including junglesop. Each ape distributes about 9 tons (9 metric tons) of seeds in their lifetime.

Flowering lianas are woody vines. This one began as a shrub, rooted in the earth, but now its elongated stems twine upward over tree-supports to reach the light.

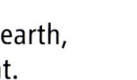

Okapis are giraffes' only relatives. They eat succulent leaves of plants that are especially abundant in tree-fall light gaps.

Elusive *forest francolins* are secretive and hard to spot. They prefer to live inside the rainforest hidden from predators by dense vegetation.

Miracle fruit

Congo cockatoo

Junglesop

Honeycomb fungus

Fire skink

Fern

Hungry *red-tailed ant-thrushes* hunt near or on the ground and often follow driver ant swarms picking off the fleeing insects one by one.

Polypore fungi grow on old trees and consume decaying wood. They break down the wood, playing an important role in the recycling of rainforest nutrients.

The ancestors of *Fiji banded iguanas* live in far-flung South America, and probably arrived on floating vegetation riding westward on currents that swept across the Pacific.

The only mammal species unique to Taveuni, the *Fijian monkey-faced bat* descended from bats that over flew from Australasia. Its tiny population is critically endangered.

Found only in Taveuni, *Tagimoucia* bears striking hanging clusters of crimson and white blooms. It is the national flower of Fiji.

Some of the world's biggest millipedes live in Fiji. *Giant millipedes* feed on leaf litter and can grow to 8 in (20 cm).

Spear palm

Karawa

Taveuni silktail

Red-tipped fern

Orange-breasted myzomela

The *Pacific tree boa* preys on birds and bats—catching them at night and killing by constriction. Unlike most reptiles, it doesn't lay eggs but gives birth to live young.

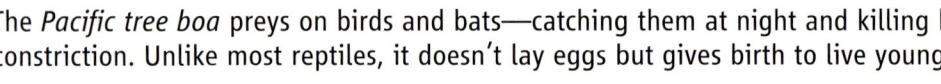

Northern wattled honeyeaters probe flowers for nectar—helping to pollinate many of them. They prefer to stay in the trees searching out the sweetest flowers.

The "pick-pick" call of the fruit-eating *orange dove*, said to sound like drops falling into a sink, is very different from the cooing of more familiar pigeons.

The *Fiji woodswallow* sweeps through the air to catch insects on the wing—then uses its chunky bill to pull prey apart when back at the perch.

ISOLATED WORLD
Bouma National Heritage Park, Taveuni Island, Fiji

A wet season afternoon in Bouma's remote tropical rainforest sees wildlife emerging from a passing storm. Just a few million years ago, this Fijian island was nothing but bare rock cooling from a mid-ocean volcanic eruption. Since then, a rainforest has grown up from spores, seeds, and animals dispersing here by air or sea—and evolving into new species found nowhere else on Earth.

Euodia hortensis

Collared lory

Coconut palm

Giant forest gecko

Red ginger

The woody nuts of salt-tolerant *coconut palms* float when washed out to sea and survive long enough to germinate on beaches.

Female *platymantis frogs* lay their eggs on the leaves of screw pines and palms. The eggs hatch into tiny froglets rather than tadpoles.

Most crabs cannot survive long on land, but *purple land crabs* use their gills like lungs to breathe in air, helping them live in the moist forest.

Ucikau walking sticks are giant insects that can grow as long as a child's arm! They have fragile legs—if one is broken off by a predator, another will grow in its place.

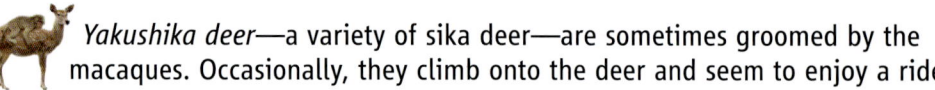 *Yakushika deer*—a variety of sika deer—are sometimes groomed by the macaques. Occasionally, they climb onto the deer and seem to enjoy a ride.

 Webs built by female *golden silk orb-weavers*—or giant wood spiders— are yellow. The largest can measure a staggering 6.5 ft (2 m) across.

FAIRY-TALE FOREST
Yakushima National Park, Japan

It's springtime on Yakushima Island, the wettest place in Japan. This mysterious warm-temperate rainforest has shady moss-covered valleys, deer-riding macaques, and a fungus that looks like it belongs on a coral reef. The National Park is home to some of Japan's most ancient trees. One giant cedar, known as Jōmon Sugi, has a trunk 13 ft (4 m) wide and is thought to be 7,000 years old.

Yakushima cedar

The *Ryukyu robin* likes to sing from a low perch in the shade. A pair can raise three clutches of eggs each season.

In spring, the *Japanese sapphireberry* blossom falls like confetti. In fall, the macaques feast on the blue fruit.

Japanese weasel

  *Common mapwing butterflies* have an unpredictable flight. They zigzag and suddenly change direction to make it difficult for birds to catch them.

 Female *small Japanese field mice* give birth to a large brood of young because they are constantly preyed upon by raccoon dogs and Japanese weasels.

 *Japanese raccoon dogs* are not native to Yakushima but were introduced to the island by humans. The species is an opportunistic omnivore that eats most things.

Black paradise flycatchers migrate to Yakushima forest every spring to breed. They spend the rest of the year on mainland Asia.

Southern Japanese hemlocks can grow up to 100 ft (30 m). Their cones can remain on the tree for several years.

Japanese sparrowhawks are swift, secretive hunters that use their speed to catch small birds, mammals, or reptiles inside the forest.

Japanese white-eye

Yakushima coral fungus

Japanese tiger beetle

Whistling green pigeon

 A *cobra lily* has a dark head shaped like the hood of an angry cobra snake about to strike. It thrives in a shady, damp location.

 *Yakushima macaques* live in groups. They renew their social bonds by mutual grooming (or allogrooming)—each cleaning the fur of another.

Bald uakaris are flooded forest specialists. They can travel through the treetops without coming down to the ground for months until the floodwaters recede.

Buriti palms need wet habitats, thriving in swamps and flooded rainforest. Their fruit is an important source of food for many animal species.

A relative of the pine marten, *tayras* are adaptable omnivores, constantly on the move in search of prey such as small mammals.

Goeldi's marmosets like to eat fungi. During the dry season, they feed on fungus that grows on rotting logs left by the floods.

THE FLOODED FOREST
Iquitos várzea, Brazil

The várzea is a tropical lowland rainforest of extreme change. Wet season floods cover huge areas of Amazonian forest, forcing animals that inhabit the forest floor to leave to find drier land, while others climb into the canopy. Fish swim among the trees until the rainfall slows. The floods recede and young plants spring from the earth until the rains return.

Patawa palm

Collared tree runner

White-chinned jacamar

Giant philodendron

Rainforest *butterflies* can be seen "mud-puddling." The puddles contain rotting plant and animal material that offer vital salts and minerals to the butterflies.

The diet of *white-lipped peccaries* is varied. Fruit is a favorite, but they also eat nuts, earthworms, eggs, and even dead animals.

Amazon river dolphins are gray at birth but become pink as they grow. The color allows them to see each other in the dark floodwater.

Solitary *margays* have a special kind of rotatable ankle joint that helps them climb headfirst down tree trunks and branches.

Silver arowana swim close to the water surface and jump out to catch prey in midair. They eat insects, small birds, and even bats.

Peculiarly for a forest-dwelling bird, *hoatzins* are leaf-eaters. They have a digestive system like that of cows, which breaks down leaves.

Blue-headed parrot

Redtail catfish

Tambaqui

Ocellate river stingray

Angel fish

Amazon manatees live in the water but need to breathe air. Their nostrils close automatically when grazing on underwater plants in the floodwaters.

Neon tetras are distant cousins of piranhas. They like to stick to shallow creeks where water is stained brown by tannins coming from fallen leaf litter.

RAINFOREST PLANTS AND FUNGI

Rainforests are home to more than half of the world's species of plants. As well as being hot spots of biodiversity, these lush habitats influence local weather, help produce the oxygen we breathe, and are the sources of some life-saving medicines. But rainforests are also fragile places that need protecting today as much as ever before. Here is a selection of some of the remarkable plants and fungi that feature on the pages of this book.

DAINTREE, AUSTRALIA (see pages 4–5)

WILD BANANA
Unlike bananas grown by farmers, the fruits of this species are shorter, reddish when ripe, and grow in upright-pointing clusters, instead of hanging downward.

VELVET LEAF
Named for its hairy leaves that feel like velvet to the touch, this shrub produces berries that are eaten by birds. The plant is the source of medicine that can treat inflammation.

BUMPY SATINASH
This tree is called "bumpy" because its flowers and fruits sprout directly from the trunk, rather than from ends of thin shoots.

TANJUNG PUTING NATIONAL PARK, INDONESIA (see pages 6–7)

MENGGARIS TREE
These trees are among the tallest in Asian rainforests, emerging above the canopy and supported by buttressed trunks. High branches provide nesting sites for giant honeybees, well away from ground predators.

RAMIN
Ramin trees thrive in shaded swampy forests where the canopy is lower. They have very few branches on their lower trunk, making it difficult for most animals to climb.

KERUING
Asian rainforests are dominated by a family of lofty, flowering trees called dipterocarps, such as keruing. Their trunks are valued as building material and is the cause of much deforestation.

TONGASS NATIONAL FOREST, US (see pages 8–9)

WESTERN RED HEMLOCK
Hemlocks that live for more than 1,000 years and grow to 230 ft (70 m) are among the many species of conifers that dominate the damp, evergreen forests along the Pacific coast of North America.

WESTERN COLUMBINE
Growing on moist riverbanks, the red flowers and abundant sweet nectar of this plant attract hummingbirds that are its main pollinators.

DEVIL'S CLUB
Indigenous people have long recognized the medicinal properties of this large-leaved plant—its bark and roots have been used to treat headaches, colds, and even tuberculosis, an infection of the lungs.

MAKIRA NATURAL PARK, MADAGASCAR (see pages 10–11)

BIRD'S NEST FERN
This fern grows on the ground and on trees, but unlike the finely divided fronds of most ferns, the leaves of this species are broad and leathery—helping it tolerate drier conditions perched on high branches.

MALAGASY TEA
A health-giving traditional tea is made from the leaves of this plant. The roots have been used to treat humans with stomach worms.

TRAVELER'S TREE
Although resembling a palm, this plant is more closely related to bananas and ginger. Rainwater collecting in its leaf bases helps sustain thirsty travelers.

MANÚ NATIONAL PARK, PERU (see pages 12–13)

WILD FIG
Fig seeds dropped by fruit-eating birds and monkeys germinate in the crowns of other trees—then strangle their "hosts" by sending woody roots down to the ground.

BROMELIAD
Bromeliads are members of the pineapple family and grow as epiphytes in the rainforests. Many are able to store water in tightly overlapping leaves at their bases.

AGUAJE PALM
This enormous palm thrives on the swampy land of the Amazon basin. Its fruit are eaten by macaws, and its seeds disperse by floating on water.

VOLCANOES NATIONAL PARK, RWANDA (see pages 14–15)

GIANT GROUNDSEL
This plant is a giant cousin of the groundsels and ragworts that are better known as garden weeds elsewhere in the world. They grow on the slopes of the Virunga volcanoes and can reach 20 ft (6 m).

GIANT HEATHER
This tree-sized relative of moorland heathers grows in subalpine regions above the montane rainforest treeline, where it thrives on dry, shallow soils.

AFRICAN REDWOOD
With their short, thick trunks, these trees dominate montane forests—growing less than half of the height of canopy trees in lowland rainforests.

TAMAN NEGARA NATIONAL PARK, MALAYSIA (see pages 16–17)

RAMBUTAN
Rambutan trees have sweet and juicy fruit. Their name derives from the local word for "hair" and describes the tiny spines that cover each fruit.

SEALING WAX PALM
The name of this plant comes from the red coverings of young leaves that reminded people of the wax used to seal letters in the 16th century.

PAGODA FLOWER
Pagoda blooms are made up of hundreds of tiny flowers. Each contains a large store of nectar that attracts pollinating insects from around the forest.

RAKIURA NATIONAL PARK, NEW ZEALAND (see pages 18–19)

BUSH LAWYER
The bush lawyer plant produces tasty berries, but the tangled vines are covered with sharp, hooked thorns that can tear skin.

BASKET FUNGUS
The unusual latticework of this fungus produces a foul-smelling slime, which helps attract flies that disperse its spores so they can germinate elsewhere.

TREE FUCHSIA
The nectar-rich flowers of the tree fuchsia are the largest of the world's fuchsia species. They are native to New Zealand and grow up to 100 ft (30 m) tall.

MONTEVERDE CLOUD FOREST RESERVE, COSTA RICA (see pages 20–21)

TILLANDSIA MULTICAULIS
One of many bromeliads that grow as epiphytes on cloud forest trees, this "air plant" has water-absorbing cells on its leaves to soak up moisture from the air.

WILD AVOCADO
Rare wild avocados are the favorite food of quetzals. The birds time their breeding with the ripening of the fruit and disperse the seeds throughout the forest.

PANAMANIAN OAK
Central American mountains are home to more species of oaks than anywhere else in the world. Some are evergreen, others—like the Panamanian—lose leaves in drier seasons.

LOMAMI NATIONAL PARK, DRC (see pages 22–23)

MIRACLE FRUIT
The miracle of these berries is that they contain chemicals that coat the tongue and make bitter or sour foods taste sweet.

AFRICAN EBONY
The wood produced by this tree is almost black and was once used for the black keys on a piano. It is now a protected species.

CONGO COCKATOO
Named for its parrot-shaped flowers, this is a relative of popular garden impatiens or "busy lizzie." Its flower seed pods explode on touch to scatter the seeds.

BOUMA NATIONAL HERITAGE PARK, FIJI (see pages 24–25)

COCONUT PALM
The coconut palm grows on sun-exposed beaches at the edge of the rainforest. Its buoyant woody nuts have helped it disperse between Pacific islands.

RED GINGER
The bright red parts of ginger look like flowers, but they are really just colored leaves called bracts. The real flowers are hidden inside the bracts.

DRIFTWOOD
Fallen coastline trees can get washed into the ocean, where they float on currents—often carrying hitchhiking animals to distant islands.

YAKUSHIMA NATIONAL PARK, JAPAN (see pages 26–27)

JAPANESE CYPRESS
Japanese cypress trees smell of fresh lemon. The scent is carried long distances and is described as the "forest's perfume."

YAKUSHIMA CEDAR
Surviving on soil containing few nutrients, Yakushima cedars grow slowly but live for much longer than the Japanese cedar, which lives only for 500 years!

CORAL FUNGUS
Yakushima coral fungus is also known as "stinking earthfan." This is because it produces a smell like rotting garlic or decayed vegetation.

IQUITOS VÁRZEA, BRAZIL (see pages 28–29)

KAPOK
Among the tallest trees of the Amazon Basin, the kapok has spreading buttress roots that help support its enormous weight on soft, flood-prone ground.

GIANT PHILODENDRON
Philodendron vines climb up the trunks of trees and produce their biggest leaves high above the ground. They are popular houseplants.

PAU MULATO
This tree sheds its old bark once or twice a year, taking with it clinging vines, mosses, and lichen, and exposing new, smooth bark that has grown underneath.

MULTILAYERED HABITAT

The most complex tropical rainforests are packed with more kinds of plants than any other habitat. They grow in four layers in their scramble to reach light—from the forest floor to the tops of some of the world's tallest trees. Some animals move around the different layers while others remain inside just one.

Emergent layer

The tallest trees—some over 164 ft (50 m)—rise above the canopy to gather the most light. These "islands" in the sky are vantage points for birds of prey and animals that eat leaves and fruit.

There is little shelter from the sun, rain, and wind at the top of the emergent trees.

Canopy layer

The richest layer of all is made up of the crowns of closely packed trees and the vines and epiphytes clinging to their branches. More than 80 percent of rainforest animals live in the canopy.

Epiphytic orchids and ferns reach life-giving sunlight by growing on trees, high in the canopy.

Understory layer

Beneath the canopy are shorter trees living in heavy shade. These include palms and other species adapted to lower light, as well as younger trees waiting to grow higher.

This dark, quiet layer is a safe place for birds to nest and rear their young.

Forest floor

The most shade-tolerant plants, such as ferns, hug the forest floor, which is thick with leaf litter and dead wood. This dark place is home to animals that burrow in the ground or that do not climb.

Some animals are too heavy to climb, so they spend their lives on the forest floor.

INDEX

Amazon 2, 12–13, 28–29, 30, 31

bamboo 14
bats 7, 19, 24
bears 6, 8, 9
bees 6, 16, 30
beetles 4, 8, 11, 18, 19, 27
birds 2, 4, 5, 6, 10, 17, 18, 20, 21, 27, 29, 32
hummingbirds 8, 30
kiwis 19
bonobos 23
bromeliads 20, 30, 31
butterflies 6, 12, 20, 26, 28

caimans 12, 13
camouflage 7, 11, 12, 14, 17, 20
capybaras 12, 13
chameleons 10, 15
conservation 14, 19
crabs 25
crocodiles 4

deer 8, 26
duck-billed platypuses 4

electric eels 12
elephants 22

fish 8, 9, 12, 13, 28, 29
flowers 8, 17, 24, 30, 31
fossas 11
frogs 4, 7, 11, 20, 25
fruits 6, 16, 22, 26, 28, 30, 31
fungi 19, 23, 26, 28, 31

geckos 7, 10, 11, 25
gibbons 17
giraffe weevils 16
gorillas 14, 15

insects 7, 18, 19, 20, 23, 25, 31

jaguars 13
kangaroos 5

lemurs 10, 11
leopards 6, 22
lichen 5, 8
lizards 5, 17

macaques 16, 26, 27
macaws 12, 13, 30
manatees 29
mangabeys 22
marmosets 28
mice 26
millipedes 24
monkeys 6, 12, 14, 21, 30

okapis 23
orangutans 6, 7
orchids 4, 7, 16, 21, 32
otters 9, 12

palms 5, 25, 28, 30, 32
pangolins 22
parrots 12, 16, 19, 29
peccaries 28
penguins 18
piranhas 13

racoon dogs 26, 27
river dolphins 29

seeds 4, 5, 8, 16, 21, 22, 23, 30, 31
sloths 13, 21
slugs 19
snakes 7, 13, 16, 24
spiders 5, 10, 11, 26
squirrels 15, 16, 20

temperate forests 2, 3, 8–9, 18–19, 26–27
tenrecs 11
tigers 17
toucans 21
trees 2, 3, 9, 16, 22, 27, 30, 31, 32
ancient 5, 26
tropical forests 2, 3, 4–7, 12–17, 22–25, 28–29, 32
turtles 12

vines 11, 22, 23, 31, 32

wolves 8

plants 2, 11, 30–31, 32

ACKNOWLEDGMENTS

Dorling Kindersley would like to thank:
Sheila Collins and Simon Mumford for additional design; Ed Pearce for additional editing; Carron Brown for proofreading and the index; Sakshia Saluja for picture research; Steve Crozier for creative retouching; Mik Gates and Rob Perry for visualization

The publisher would also like to thank the following for their kind permission to reproduce their photographs:

(Key: a-above; b-below/bottom; c-centre; f-far; l-left; r-right; t-top)
2-3 Bioscience: An Ecoregions-Based Approach to Protecting Half the Terrestrial Realm DOI: https://doi.org/10.1093/biosci/bix014 Licensed under CC-BY 4.0. 4-5 Dorling Kindersley: Andrew Beckett @ Illustration X / Alamy Stock Photo: Dave Watts (southern cassowary) / Corbis: L. Clarke(ripples), Shutterstock.com: attem (forest), c 1959 (banana tree), FiledIMAGE (river), Ken Griffiths (kangaroo), Keung (beetle), Jakub Maculewicz (palm), Lee ArtPhotos (palm), Sergey Uryadnikov (monkeys), Imogen Warren (fruit-dove and pademelon), Brooke Whatnall (river), worldswildlifewonders (platypus). 6-7 Dorling Kindersley: Andrew Beckett @ Illustration X / Shutterstock.com: Agus_Tri1975 (monkey), Jiri Balek (forest), Binturong-tonoscarpe (durian tree), Globetrottersbucketlist (orangutan), Dr_Flash, Clive Gibson, David Havel and Sergey Uryadnikov (proboscis monkeys), Eric Isselee (leopard), keywordphil (bats), NaturesMomentsuk (mother and baby), imran nugraha (trees), Larwin, nasidastudio, RRizki, Sifrx90 Photography and Mr. Jirakrit Sittiwong. 8-9 Dorling Kindersley: Chris Smith - KJA Artists. 10-11 Dorling Kindersley: Sofian Moumene / Artstation: Artyom Polovyanov / Dreamstime.com: Michael Sheehan (dung beetle) / Maxtree / naturepl.com: Nick Garbutt (vontsira fur texture) / quixel.com. 12-13 Dorling Kindersley: Andrew Beckett @ Illustration X / Dreamstime.com Brooke Parish (sloth), Getty Images / iStock: ViniSouza128 (palm trees). 14-15 Dorling Kindersley: Andrew Beckett @ Illustration X / Alamy Stock Photo: José María Barres Manuel (tree), Shutterstock: Tony Campbell (golden monkey), jpreat (palm), K I Photography (rock), Joe McDonald, Mary Ann McDonald and Ariane Ribbeck (gorilla), Tetyana Dotsenko, Mohamad alias, Radzimy, The Road Provides and Travel Stock (vegetation), Robert Harding Video (spurfowl). 16-17 Dorling Kindersley: Andrew Beckett @ Illustration X / Alamy Stock Photo: Steffen Hauser / botanikfoto (bauhinia kockiana), Shutterstock: Lam Van Linh (Burmese grape), Martine Liu 58 (buzzard), Barbarajo and Taweesak Sriwannawit (flower), George87 (gaur), Thipwan, Jeng Bo Yuan and songwut tanoi (gibbon), Tanes Ngamsom (hornbill), jpreat (palm), Mohamad alias (plant), Yuawalida Wong (squirrel), JF507 (tiger), Natural Mosart, Mas Bowo photo, H-AB Photograph, ThamKC, kamontad999 and Haris_1981 (trees), YapAhock (trogon). 18-19 Dorling Kindersley: Andrew Beckett @ Illustration X / Alamy Stock Photo: Paul R. Sterry / Nature Photographers Ltd (Kererü), Marko König / imageBROKER.com GmbH & Co. KG (parakeet), Shutterstock: Peter Gudella and Photos BrianScantlebury (beach), Imogen Warren (cuckoo), roycy fernandes (kererü), Victor Baril, Robert CHG and Patrick Weis (penguins), tonytao (tree), Relic74, Polglish.pl, Tonia Kraakman and Heather Joy (vegetation), Martin Pelanek (weka). 20-21 Dorling Kindersley: Chris Smith - KJA Artists / Adobe Stock: Molinero de Gúdar (avocado fruit). 22-23 Dorling Kindersley: Chris Smith - KJA Artists / Dreamstime.com: Lukas Blazek. 24-25 Dorling Kindersley: Sofian Moumene / Maxtree (alpinia purpurata, coconut tree, hibiscus), quixel.com: megascan (rocks) / Globe Plants (screwpine). 26-27 Dorling Kindersley: Sofian Moumene, Andrew Beckett @ Illustration X (deers) / Dreamstime.com: Sergey Uryadnikov (monkey) / Getty Images / iStock: apple2499 (mountain) / Shutterstock: ErikMandre (racoon) / 3dsky: AlexHappy (moss) / Globe Plants (plants), quixel.com: megascan (rocks), Sketchfab: xfrog (trees). 28-29 Dorling Kindersley: Andrew Beckett @ Illustration X / Shutterstock.com: Praisaeng (angelfish), Duck Stock (catfish), Tristan Barrington (hoatzin), CampSmoke (mushrooms), Elly Miller (peccary), jular seesulai, LeoGM, guentermanaus, Claudio Morini, Robert Harding Video and GTW (trees), Allexxandar and Patricia Funke Batista (under water), Dr Morley Read, Rostislav Stefanek and (vegetation). 30 123RF.com: georgeburba (ca). Alamy Stock Photo: MJ Photography (crb). Depositphotos Inc: luckypic (ca/Tree). Dreamstime.com: Siti Maryam Mohd. Arifin (ca/Keruing Padi); Gerold Grotelueschen (cla); Arkadij Schell (cb); Redfinch (bl); Taechit Tanantornanutra (cr); Augustin Soulard (cb/Aphloia theiformis); Gan Chaonan (cb/palm tree); Tom Meaker (bc/erica arborea); Salparadis (bc/Mount Kenya). Getty Images / iStock: Gerald Corsi (c). Shutterstock.com: Muslianshah Masrie (cra); Daniel Toh (ca/Syzygium cormiflorum). 31 Adobe Stock: Molinero de Gúdar (fcra). Alamy Stock Photo: David Keith Jones / Images of Africa Photobank (clb). Depositphotos Inc: Aisyaqilumar (fcla); kelpfish (ca); robert.buchel.fl1.li (cb); Southtownboy (cra). Dreamstime.com: Sarfraz Ahmad (c); Foto76 (cla); David Williams (cb/Cyprus tree); Ken Griffiths (bc); Gary Webber (ca/Basket fungus). Getty Images / iStock: Matt Anderson (crl); KKKvintage (bl); Lakeview_Images (ca/Fuchsia excorticata); Travel_Motion (ca/Capirona amazon tall); Boogich (bc/Elephant Ear Plants); simonkr (crb).

Cover images: Back: Dreamstime.com: Brooke Parish tr; Getty Images / iStock: ViniSouza128 tl

All other images © Dorling Kindersley

GLOSSARY

Arboreal
Animals that are arboreal live mainly in the trees.

Bioluminescent
A living thing that can produce and emit light.

Camouflage
The color or pattern of a living thing that blends in with its environment so that it can't be seen.

Carnivore
An animal that eats meat.

Ecosystem
A community of living things that interact with each other and their environment.

Epiphyte
A plant that grows on another plant and takes in moisture and nutrients from rain and water vapor through its leaves and aerial roots.

Germinate
A process in which a seed or a spore begins to sprout and grow into a new plant.

Invertebrate
An animal with no backbone, such as an insect, spider, and crab.

Lichen
An organism that is a partnership between an alga and a fungus, and which share a body.

Marsupial
A mammal whose babies are born underdeveloped, and which are typically nurtured in a pouch.

Nocturnal
Animals that are active during the night.

Omnivore
An animal that eats both plants and other animals.

Photosynthesis
The process by which plants use the sun's energy to make their own food from carbon dioxide and water.

Pollination
The way pollen is moved, usually by wind or animals, from one flower to another in order to reproduce.

Prehensile
A part of the body that is adapted for grasping or wrapping around a branch. A prehensile tail can support the entire weight of the body.

Primate
A mammal group that includes apes, monkeys, and humans.

Subalpine
The slopes of a mountain just above the tree line.

Temperate
A region between the equator and the poles without extremes of climate; it has warm summers and cold winters, and high rainfall.

Tropical
A region around the equator with a warm or hot climate year-round and with abundant rainfall or pronounced dry season.